CHESTER'S EA
CAROLS

by Carol Barratt

1. We Wish You A Merry Christmas
2. Jolly Old Saint Nicholas
3. Jingle Bells
4. Christmas Morning (A Piano Solo)
5. Good King Wenceslas
6. Silent Night
7. As Each Happy Christmas
8. Christmas Is Coming
9. Away In A Manger
10. Infant Holy, Infant Lowly
11. Once In Royal David's City
12. We Three Kings
13. The First Nowell
14. While Shepherds Watched
15. See Amid The Winter's Snow
16. It Came Upon The Midnight Clear
17. Hark! The Herald Angels Sing
18. As With Gladness Men Of Old
19. O Come, All Ye Faithful
20. Ding Dong! Merrily On High
21. The Holly And The Ivy

Exclusive distributors:

Chester Music
(A division of Music Sales Limited)
8/9 Frith Street, London W1V 5TZ.

This book © Copyright 1990 Chester Music
Order No.CH59121
ISBN 0.7119.2441.4

Music processed by Barnes Music Engraving

Printed in the United Kingdom by
Caligraving Limited, Thetford, Norfolk.

Chester Music Limited
(A division of Music Sales Limited)

These Carols have been arranged as simply as possible,
and the range is just right for the child's hands *and* voice.

They progress as follows:

Nos. 1 and 2 - alternating hands (plus piano accompaniments)
Nos. 3 and 4 - hands together in set 5-finger hand positions
Nos. 5 to 11 - right hand out of set position,
left hand in set 5-finger hand position
Nos. 12 to 22 - both hands out of set hand positions

Enjoy yourselves!

Happy Christmas

Carol Barratt

The chord symbols suggested have been chosen to suit the solo melody
and do not always correspond with the harmony of the arrangements, as importance
has been placed on left hand accompaniments using simple hand positions.

1.
WE WISH YOU A MERRY CHRISTMAS

2.
JOLLY OLD SAINT NICHOLAS

Accompaniment

American

Jol - ly old Saint Nich - o - las, Lean your ear this way,

D   A7   Bm   F#m

Don't you tell a sin - gle soul What I'm going to say;

G   D   E7   A

Christ - mas Eve is com - ing soon, Now, you dear old man,

D   A7   Bm   F#m

Whis - per what you'll bring to me, Tell me, if you can.

G   D   A7   D

3. JINGLE BELLS
An American Song

J. Pierpont

4.
CHRISTMAS MORNING
A Piano Solo

With excitement!

Carol Barratt

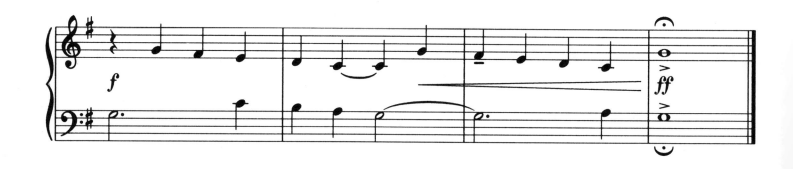

5.
GOOD KING WENCESLAS

From now on the right hand does not stay in a set position.
To help you with these changes of hand position, look for
the ★ sign which shows you when the hand has a 'big' move.

English

6.

SILENT NIGHT

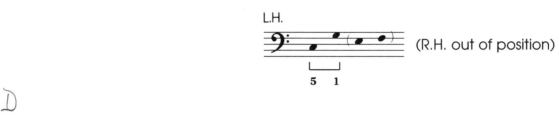

German

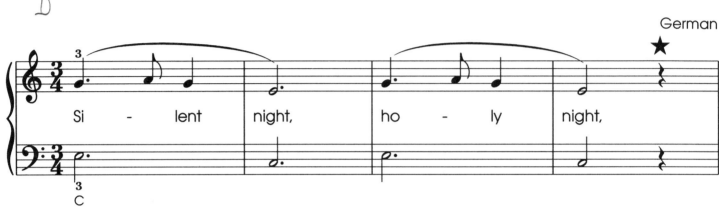

Si - lent night, ho - ly night,

C

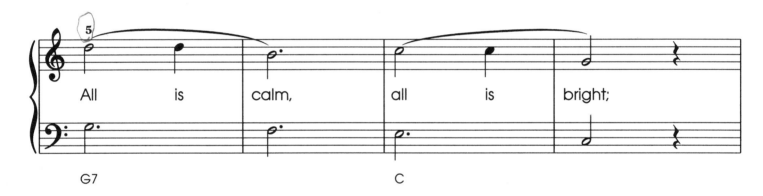

All is calm, all is bright;

G7   C

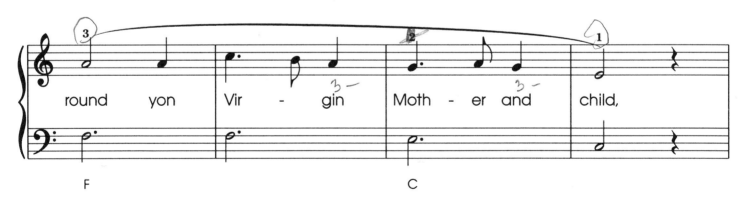

round yon Vir - gin Moth - er and child,

F   C

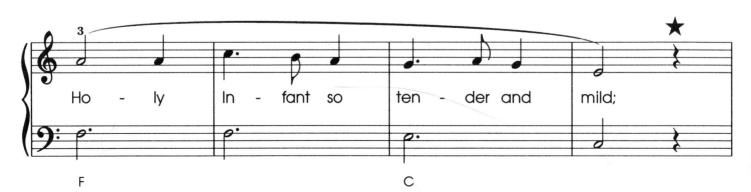

Ho - ly In - fant so ten - der and mild;

F   C

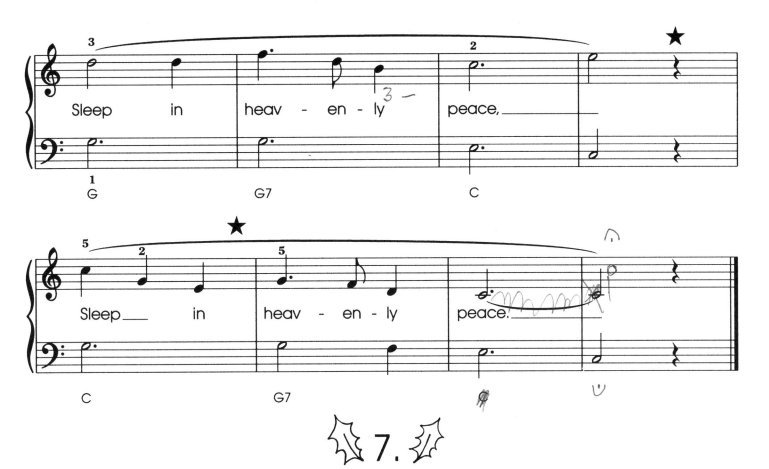

Sleep in heav - en - ly peace,

Sleep in heav - en - ly peace.

7.
AS EACH HAPPY CHRISTMAS

L.H.

(R.H. out of position)

5 1

German

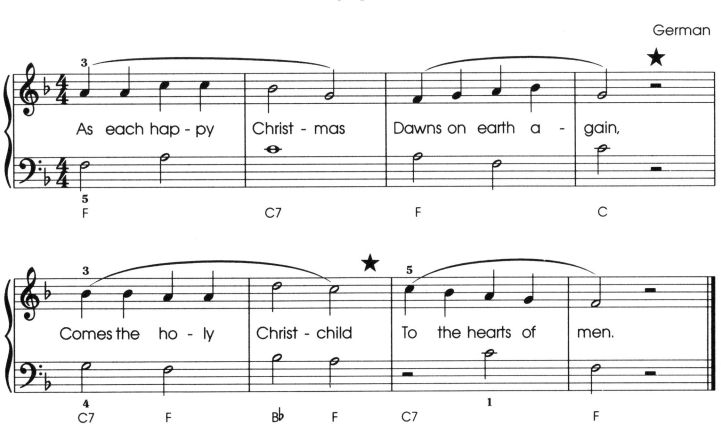

As each hap - py Christ - mas Dawns on earth a - gain,

Comes the ho - ly Christ - child To the hearts of men.

8.
CHRISTMAS IS COMING

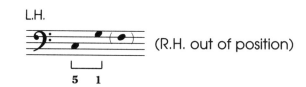

If you feel that you still need the ★ sign to help you with changing hand positions, add it yourself where there is a difficult move.

9.
AWAY IN A MANGER

L.H. (R.H. out of position)

A - way in a__ man-ger, no__ crib for a bed, The__

F   C7   F   Dm   Gm

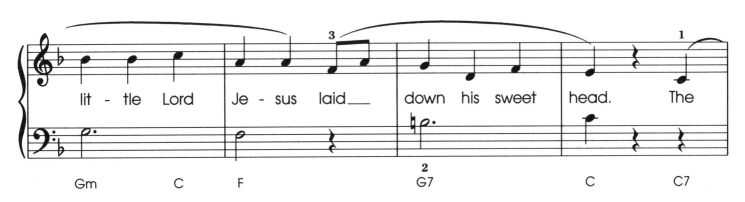

lit - tle Lord Je - sus laid__ down his sweet head. The

Gm   C   F   G7   C   C7

stars in the__ bright sky looked__ down where He lay, The__

F   C7   F   Dm   Gm

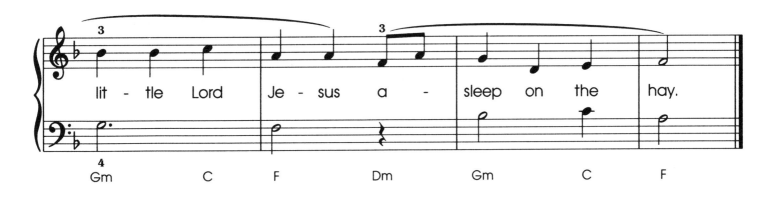

lit - tle Lord Je - sus a - sleep on the hay.

Gm   C   F   Dm   Gm   C   F

10.
INFANT HOLY, INFANT LOWLY

11.
ONCE IN ROYAL DAVID'S CITY

English

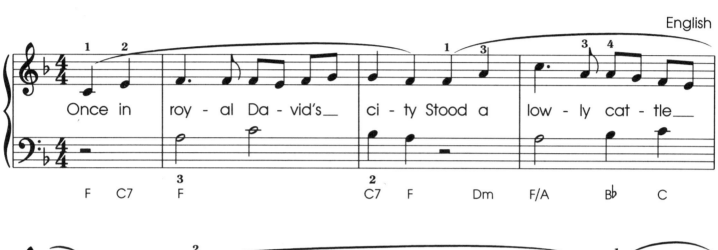

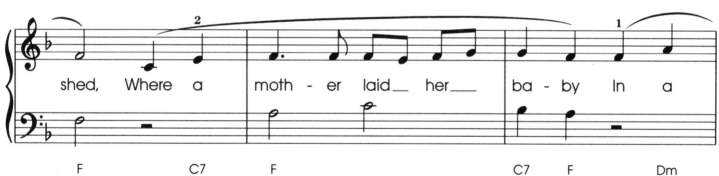

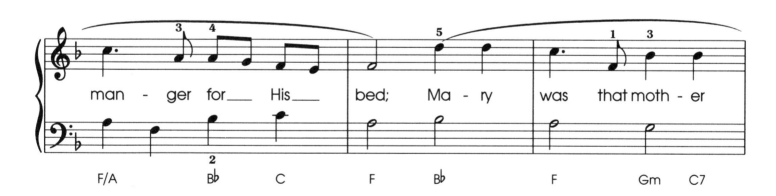

12.
WE THREE KINGS

From now on, **both** hands are out of set 5-finger hand positions.

American

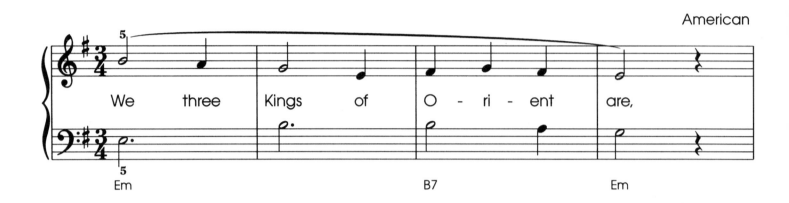

We three Kings of O - ri - ent are,

Em   B7   Em

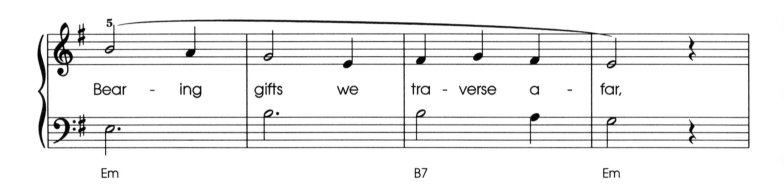

Bear - ing gifts we tra - verse a - far,

Em   B7   Em

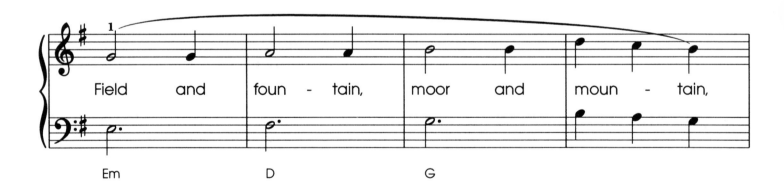

Field and foun - tain, moor and moun - tain,

Em   D   G

Chorus

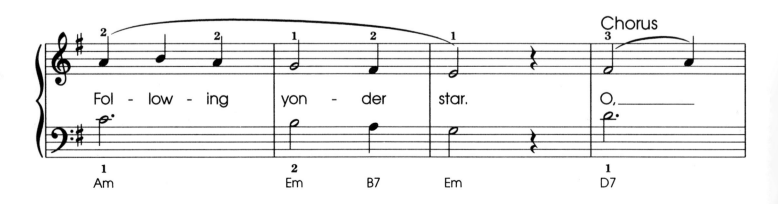

Fol - low - ing yon - der star.   O, _____

Am   Em   B7   Em   D7

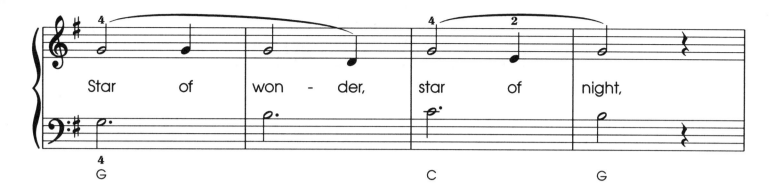

Star   of   won - der,   star   of   night,

G   C   G

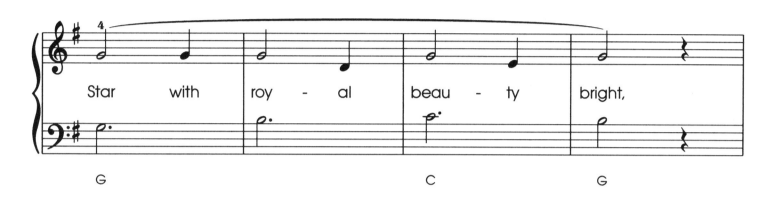

Star   with   roy - al   beau - ty   bright,

G   C   G

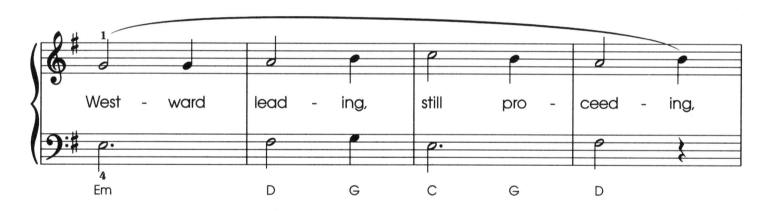

West - ward   lead - ing,   still   pro - ceed - ing,

Em   D   G   C   G   D

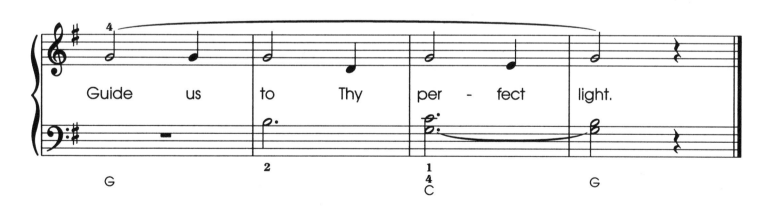

Guide   us   to   Thy   per - fect   light.

G   C   G

13.
THE FIRST NOWELL

English

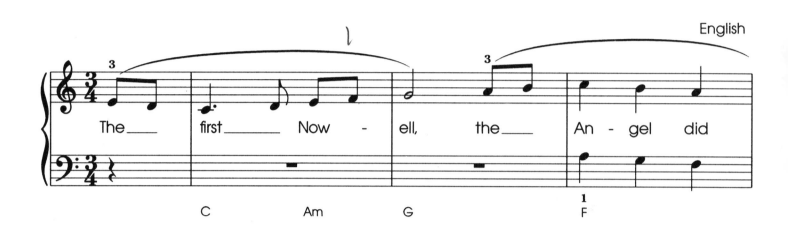

The___ first_____ Now - ell, the___ An - gel did

C   Am   G   F

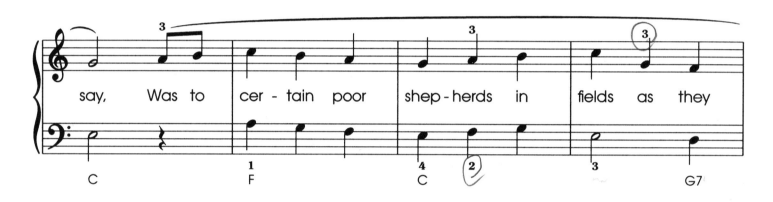

say, Was to cer - tain poor shep-herds in fields as they

C   F   C   G7

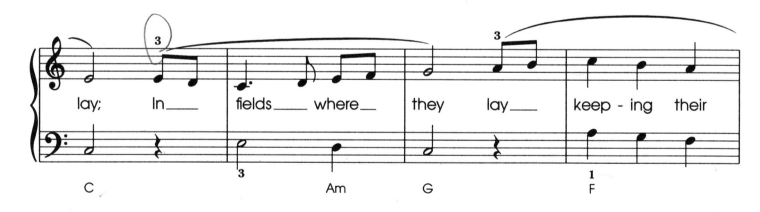

lay; In___ fields___ where___ they lay___ keep - ing their

C   Am   G   F

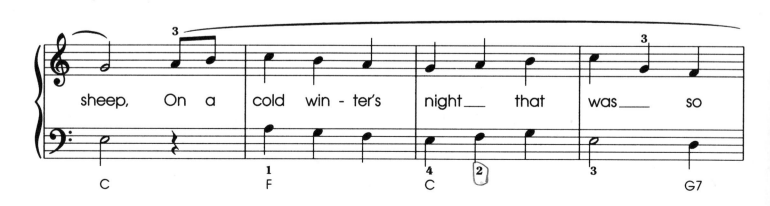

sheep, On a cold win - ter's night___ that was___ so

C   F   C   G7

14.
WHILE SHEPHERDS WATCHED

English (Este's Psalter 1592)

15.
SEE AMID THE WINTER'S SNOW

English

See a-mid the win-ter's snow, Born for us on earth be-low,

G   C   G   C   G/D   D

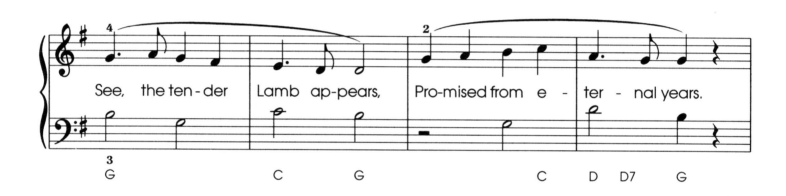

See, the ten-der Lamb ap-pears, Pro-mised from e-ter-nal years.

G   C   G   C D D7 G

Chorus

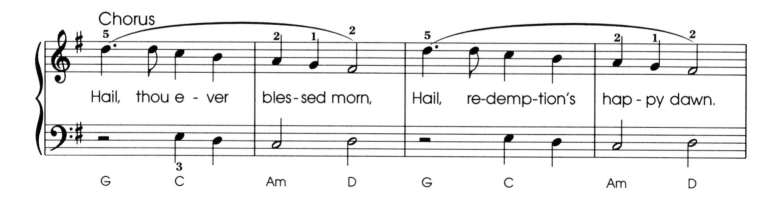

Hail, thou e-ver bles-sed morn, Hail, re-demp-tion's hap-py dawn.

G   C   Am D   G   C   Am D

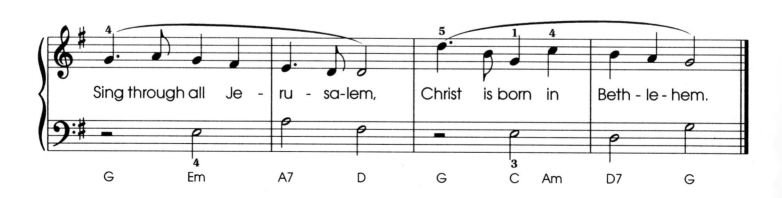

Sing through all Je-ru-sa-lem, Christ is born in Beth-le-hem.

G   Em A7 D   G   C Am D7 G

16.
IT CAME UPON THE MIDNIGHT CLEAR

English

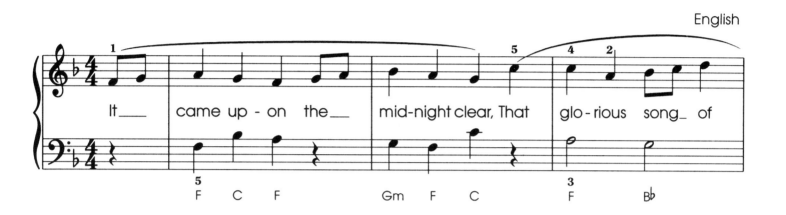

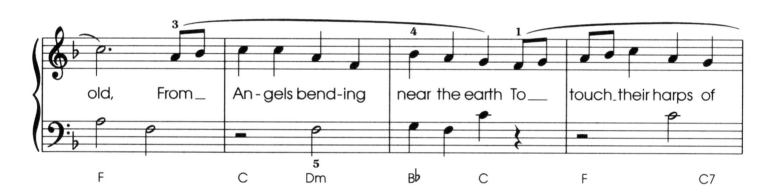

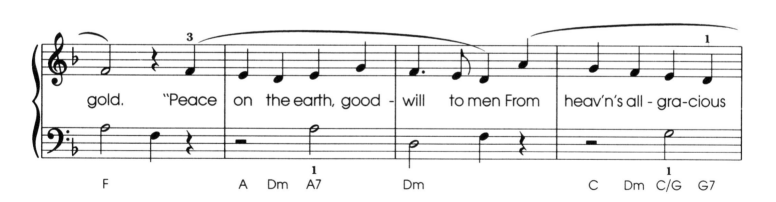

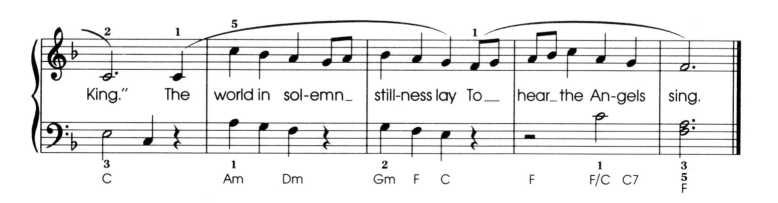

17.
HARK! THE HERALD ANGELS SING

F. Mendelssohn

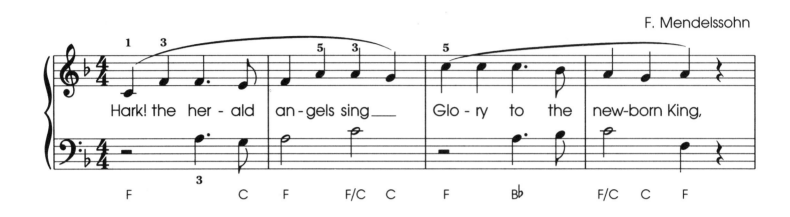

Hark! the her - ald an - gels sing___ Glo - ry to the new-born King,

F   C   F   F/C C   F   Bb   F/C C   F

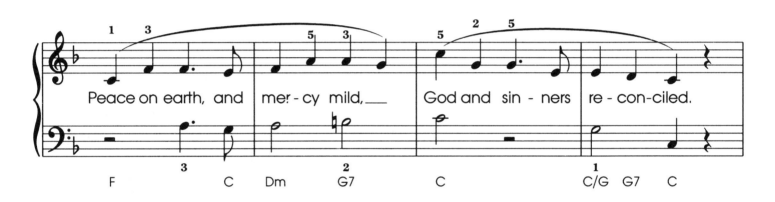

Peace on earth, and mer - cy mild,___ God and sin - ners re - con-ciled.

F   C   Dm   G7   C   C/G G7 C

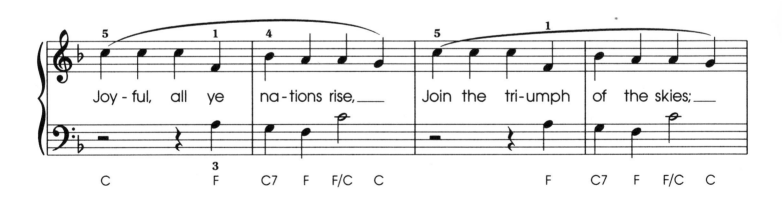

Joy - ful, all ye na - tions rise,___ Join the tri-umph of the skies;___

C   F   C7 F   F/C C   F   C7 F   F/C C

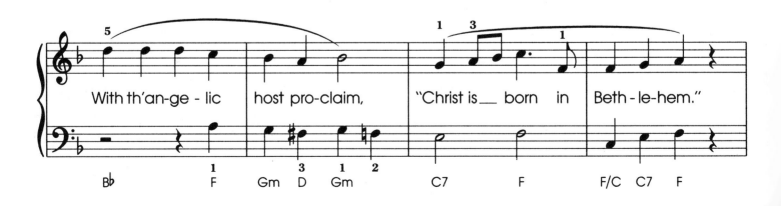

With th'an-ge - lic host pro-claim, "Christ is__ born in Beth - le-hem."

Bb   F   Gm D   Gm   C7   F   F/C C7 F

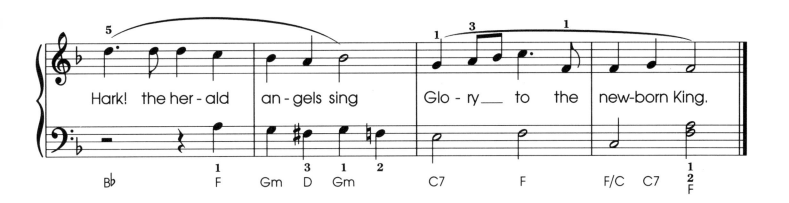

Hark! the her-ald an-gels sing Glo-ry___ to the new-born King.

Bb | F | Gm D Gm | C7 | F | F/C C7 | 1. 2. F

18.
AS WITH GLADNESS MEN OF OLD

German

As with_glad-ness men of old Did the guid-ing star be-hold,

G | D | G C | G | C | G C | G/D D7 | G

As with_ joy they hailed its light, Lead-ing on-ward, beam-ing bright:

G | D | G C | G | C | G C | G/D D7 | G

So, most gra-cious Lord may we Ev - er-more be led to Thee.

G | D | G | C | G C | G/D D7 | G

19.
O COME, ALL YE FAITHFUL

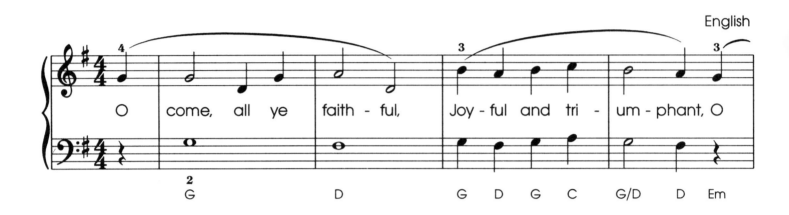

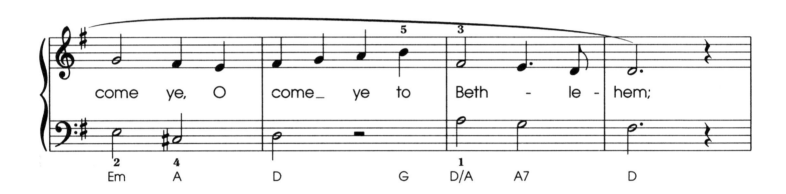

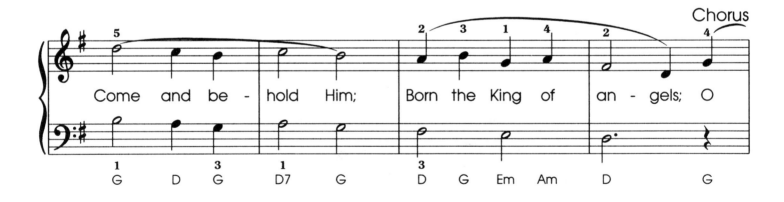

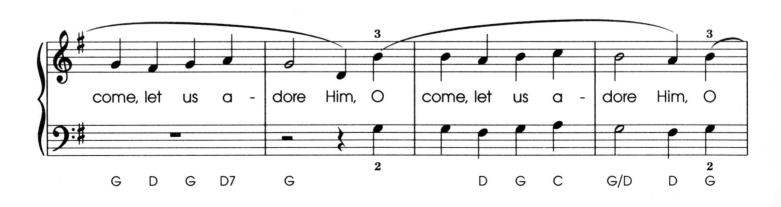

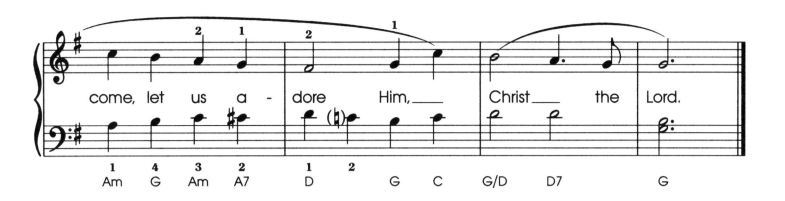

come, let us a - dore Him, ___ Christ ___ the Lord.

Am   G   Am   A7   D   G   C   G/D   D7   G

20.
DING DONG! MERRILY ON HIGH

French

Ding dong! mer-ri - ly on high   In   heav'n the bells are   ring - ing;
Ding dong! ve - ri - ly the   sky   Is   riv'n with an - gels   sing - ing.

G   C6   D   G   C   Dsus   D7   G

Glo - - - - - - *ri - a, Ho - san - na in ex - cel - sis.*

D   G   C   D   B   Em   A   D

G   C   D7   G   C   Dsus   D7   G

21.
THE HOLLY AND THE IVY

English

HAPPY CHRISTMAS!